Table of Co ||||||||||

T0084931

4

Pebble®

My World

Continents
in My World

by Ella Cane

Consulting Editor: Gail Saunders-Smith, PhD

CAPSTONE PRESS
a capstone imprint

Pebble Books are published by Capstone Press,
1710 Roe Crest Drive, North Mankato, Minnesota 56003
www.capstonepub.com

Library of Congress Cataloging-in-Publication Data
Cane, Ella.
Continents in my world / by Ella Cane.
pages cm. — (Pebble books. My world.)
Includes index.
ISBN 978-1-4765-3123-6 (library binding)
ISBN 978-1-4765-3465-7 (paperback)
ISBN 978-1-4765-3471-8 (ebook pdf)
1. Continents—Juvenile literature. I. Title.
GB423.C36 2013
910.914′1—dc23   2013005992

Summary: Simple text and full-color photographs introduce the continents of the
world to the reader.

Note to Parents and Teachers

The My World set supports national curriculum standards for
social studies related to people, places, and environments. This
book describes and illustrates continents. The images support
early readers in understanding the text. The repetition of words
and phrases helps early readers learn new words. This book
also introduces early readers to subject-specific vocabulary
words, which are defined in the Glossary section. Early readers
may need assistance to read some words and to use the Table
of Contents, Glossary, Read More, Internet Sites, and Index
sections of the book.

Printed in the United States   5571

What Are Continents?

Earth is covered mostly by water. But there are huge pieces of land too. These landmasses are called continents.

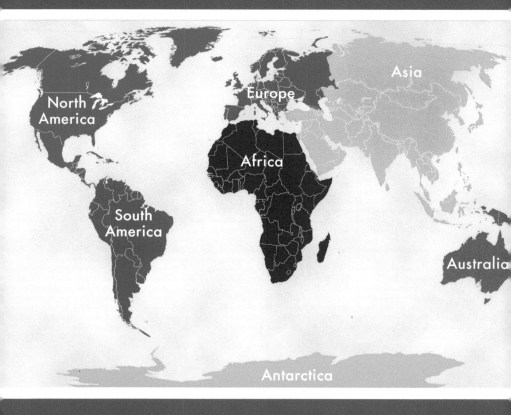

North
America

Europe

Asia

Africa

South
America

Australia

Antarctica

The world's seven continents are Asia, Africa, North America, South America, Antarctica, Europe, and Australia.

Asia

Asia is the largest continent on Earth. It also has the most people. More than 3.8 billion people live in Asia!

Africa

Africa is the second largest continent. It has the world's largest desert, the Sahara.

North America

North America is the third largest continent. Its Rocky Mountains are about 3,000 miles (4,828 kilometers) long.

South America

South America is Earth's fourth largest continent. The world's largest rain forest, the Amazon, is found there.

Antarctica

The fifth largest continent is Antarctica. It is where we find the South Pole. Antarctica is almost completely solid ice.

Europe

Europe is the sixth
largest continent.
The Alps stretch about
700 miles (1,127 km)
across Europe.

Australia

The smallest continent is Australia. A large rock called Uluru lies in central Australia. Which continent would you like to visit?

Glossary

Alps—a large mountain range in Europe

Amazon rain forest—the largest tropical rain forest in the world; it covers northern South America

desert—a dry area with little rain

rain forest—a thick forest where rain falls nearly every day

Rocky Mountains—a large mountain range in western North America; also known as the Rockies

Sahara—the largest desert in the world; it covers most of northern Africa

South Pole—the southern-most point on Earth

Uluru—a large sandstone formation in central Australia that is about 1,142 feet (348 meters) tall; also known as Ayers Rock

Read More

Kalman, Bobbie. *The ABCs of Continents.* The ABCs of the Natural World. New York: Crabtree, 2009.

Mitten, Ellen. *Counting the Continents.* Little World Geography. Vero Beach, Fla.: Rourke Pub., 2009.

Schaefer, A. R. *Spotlight on Asia.* Spotlight on the Continents. Mankato, Minn.: Capstone Press, 2011.

Internet Sites

FactHound offers a safe, fun way to find Internet sites related to this book. All of the sites on FactHound have been researched by our staff.

Here's all you do:

Visit *www.facthound.com*

Type in this code: 9781476531236

Check out projects, games and lots more at
www.capstonekids.com

Index

Word Count: 159
Grade: 1
Early-Intervention Level: 16

Editorial Credits
Shelly Lyons, editor; Juliette Peters, designer; Marcie Spence, media researcher;
Eric Manske, production specialist

Photo Credits
iStockphotos: Massimo Merlini, 20; Shutterstock: Anton Balazh, cover, Antonio
S, 18, BartlomiejMagierowski, 8, Dr. Morley Read, 14, Galyna Andrushko, 10,
Ieonello calvetti, 1, MarcelClemens, 4, Peter Kunasz, 12, Stawek, 6, Volodymyr
Goinyk, 16